MAGNIFICENT WILDERNESS

MONTANA

GEORGE WUERTHNER

FOREWORD BY BILL CUNNINGHAM

WESTCLIFFE PUBLISHERS, INC. ENGLEWOOD, COLORADO

CONTENTS

International Standard Book Number: ISBN 0-929969-40-5
Library of Congress Catalogue Card Number: 90-071518

Editor: John Fielder
Assistant Editor: Margaret Terrell Morse
Production Manager: Mary Jo Lawrence
Map: Ann W. Douden
Typographers: Dianne Borneman and Ruth Koning
Printed in Korea by Sung In Printing Company, Ltd., Seoul
Printing coordinated by Joanne Bolton, Bolton Associates, San Rafael, California
Published by Westcliffe Publishers, Inc.
2650 South Zuni Street, Englewood, Colorado 80110

Bibliography

Doig, Ivan. *English Creek*. New York: Athenium, 1984. Reprinted with permission.
Doig, Ivan. *Ride With Me, Mariah Montana*. New York: Athenium, 1990., Reprinted with permission.
Doig, Ivan. *This House of Sky*. New York: Harcourt Brace Jovanovich, Inc., 1978. Reprinted with permission.
Federal Writers' Project. *Montana, A State Guide Book*. New York: The Viking Press, 1939. Reprinted with permission.
Reprinted from *Montana Spaces*, edited by William Kittredge, © 1988 by The Montana Land Reliance, by permission of Lyons & Burford, Publishers, New York. These excerpts from "Preface" by Jan Konigsberg and "More Than Skin Deep" by Glenn Law.

First Frontispiece: Paintbrush, aster and groundsel wildflowers along Zimmer Creek, Absaroka- Beartooth Wilderness, Gallatin National Forest

Second Frontispiece: Lower Aero Lake in the Beartooth Mountains, Absaroka-Beartooth Wilderness, Gallatin National Forest

Third Frontispiece: Western hemlock dwarfed by western red cedar at Ross Creek Cedars Scenic Area, Scotchman Peak proposed wilderness, Kootenai National Forest

Title Page: Birch and cottonwood leaves on ice along the Middle Fork of the Flathead River, Flathead National Forest

Right: Limestone cliffs along the Smith River in the Little Belt Mountains, Smith River–Tenderfoot proposed wilderness, Lewis and Clark National Forest

BILL CUNNINGHAM

FOREWORD

Words prove inadequate to express my unbridled enthusiasm for this superb work of Montana wild country photography by George Wuerthner. For this collection of artful compositions has the potential to broaden the constituency for Montana's vast and varied wilderness legacy. In my mind's eye I see a thread connecting each photograph with an increase in awareness and the translation of that awareness into popular support for wild Montana. Indeed, these hidden places — large or small, rugged or gentle, remote or close — can endure only through public support.

Most of what you will marvel at in these images is wilderness in fact but, regrettably, not in law. Each landscape is compelling by virtue of its undeveloped nature. Yet most lack protection from those activities that could destroy the subtle qualities — physical and spiritual — that are their essence.

Incredibly, George captures these subtleties on film in a way that makes us feel as though we are standing by his side when the shutter opens and closes. What we've missed out on is his five-mile trek up a 70-percent slope through the predawn chill with 60 pounds of camera gear to catch the first light in an alpine meadow.

Like George, I have made Montana wildlands my passion for many years. Much of my experience has been in the political arena, as a staff member for The Wilderness Society and other conservation groups, but in recent years I've spent every available moment rambling through the spaces and places displayed on the following pages. Why? Because simply being in wild country sharpens my senses and makes me feel more alive than anywhere else.

Another reason to explore these wildlands is to be able to defend them from the heart with on-the-ground authenticity. This marvelous book is the next best thing to being there. In some ways it may be better because of an uncanny blending of technical skill and perception of quality that the photographer produces in each image. I have viewed many of these scenes on site, but I have not been able to capture them in my mind as George has through his viewfinder. For me, looking at these photographs is like seeing each subject for the first time.

You will find that each image leaves its own indelible mark, much like certain people during the course of our lives. I'll never forget my first impressions of George Wuerthner. We met in a packed hearing room in Billings during a 1977 joint House-Senate panel chaired by the late Montana Senator Lee Metcalf. George had literally backpacked across the rugged Absaroka and Beartooth mountains to Billings to testify at a forum that would help seal the fate of the million-acre Absaroka-Beartooth Wilderness. How I remember that tanned, robust figure, fresh from a hundred-mile hike, with fire in his eyes and a boundless enthusiasm energized by the tonic of wildness. The legislative battle was later won by conservationists shortly after the untimely death of Senator Metcalf.

George Wuerthner personifies the spirit that distinguishes Montana conservationists with an unmatched history of citizen activism. The key word is *tenacity* — as enduring as the wildlands that inspire such action. Until 1972, wilderness areas and boundaries were essentially decided by Forest Service bureaucrats. But the winds of populist change were blowing hard in Montana even before the 1972 passage of the Scapegoat Wilderness legislation, which was the nation's first citizen-initiated designation of wilderness.

Later, Montanans were outraged by Forest Service refusal to consider the wilderness values of nine pristine roadless areas totaling one million acres. Once again citizens took the high ground through the kind of grass-roots democracy exemplified by the Wilderness Act itself. Lee Metcalf's Montana Wilderness Study Act of 1977 forced the agency to give open-ended protection to some of the wildlands forever captured by George's lens: the deep blue Ten Lakes, the unbroken windblown crest of the Sapphires, the vast rolling forests and parks of the West Pioneers, the heartland island wilderness of the Big Snowies and more. Then came lasting protection of another million acres in the lofty Beartooth, aptly called Montana's rooftop, followed closely by the Great Bear Wilderness.

Yes, much has been accomplished, but so much more remains to be done. The vision of hope so perfectly recorded in George Wuerthner's photographs is that we will indeed muster the humility, foresight and perseverance to keep alive the soul of Montana: wild, uncluttered spaces where migratory wildlife and complex predator-prey interactions still have room to exist. We dare not set our sights any lower.

— BILL CUNNINGHAM
Frenchtown, Montana

Left: Rock outcrop near Dawson Pass looking down on Bighorn Basin and Two Medicine Lake, Glacier National Park

GEORGE WUERTHNER

PREFACE

Twenty years ago I came to Montana to study wildlife biology at the University of Montana in Missoula. Among my possessions I toted an old secondhand Pentax my dad had given me for high school graduation. Little did he or I know that someday I would make my living with a camera.

The day after my arrival in Missoula I hiked up the South Fork of Lolo Creek in the Selway-Bitterroot Wilderness, beginning my love affair with Montana and wild places. It was only natural that I began photographing the areas I visited.

Between bouts with school — it took me 12 years to get my undergraduate degrees and several more to obtain a master's — I was a "semi-professional" backpacker and wilderness wanderer. I traveled extensively throughout the West and worked as a biologist, park ranger and university instructor in a number of states, including Idaho, Wyoming, Alaska and California. And though these other places have their own allure and attractions, Montana has remained my home, with a permanent post office box and a place in my heart even when I am away.

Certainly part of my loyalty lies with the state's natural beauty. Nature has been munificent with Montana. The state wears its beauty with an easy, comfortable grace that welcomes humans even while inspiring adulation for its rugged scenery. There are still large pockets of wild, dramatic country, but at the same time the landscape is accessible and comprehendible to ordinary people with ordinary skills.

Although the western valleys — including the Bitterroot, Mission and Flathead — are among the most densely populated parts of the entire Rocky Mountain chain, Montana still has sufficient space for everyone to be neighborly, to know others across the state and to be on a first-name basis with elected representatives. There is a loyalty to the landscape — and, by association, to the people — that is seldom found elsewhere. This loyalty has inspired some to call Montana "the last best place."

Montana is one state, but it is really three major geographical regions rolled into one. Each has its boosters and adherents claiming their section to be the best of the last best place. I've rambled among the alpine summits of the Beartooths, trodden the lush forests of the Cabinets, floated the wild stretches of the Missouri Breaks and climbed the peaks of the Bitterroots. To pick a favorite would be like asking parents to choose which son or daughter they like best.

Montana's northwestern corner is more like the heavily forested ranges of British Columbia than the wide open, arid West. Mountain ranges jumble together, almost blending into one another — the Cabinet Mountains, Swan Range, Whitefish Range, Purcell Mountains. Draining the deep snowfields of these uplands are a myriad of clear, cold creeks and streams all converging to form rivers — the Clark Fork, North Fork of the Flathead, Yaak, Kootenai. These big, brawling rivers race through narrow, densely forested valleys of western red cedar, western white pine, western hemlock and western larch. In the understory and among the forest boughs thrive plant and animal species more indicative of a Pacific Northwest coastal rain forest than a region of Montana.

Here, too, is Glacier National Park, one of the crown jewels of the National Park System and a major drawing card for Montana's growing tourism industry. Ironic as it may seem today, when a national park was first proposed here, the local people, including the Kalispell Chamber of Commerce, were opposed to it. There was talk of developing oil and timber reserves in what is now the park, and the idea that preserving scenery and wildlife has more value than the economic opportunities associated with development was a lesson not yet learned. But if we were to add up the monetary benefits of the nearly 90 years of tourism attracted primarily by Glacier, that revenue would easily amount to far greater wealth than development could have ever brought.

Unfortunately, we still hear that same short-sighted opposition to more wilderness designation and wildlife habitat preservation. The lessons of the past too frequently do not become guideposts for the future.

Moving south and east in the state, into the headwaters of the Missouri River, the intervening mountains begin to wring out the moisture from the Pacific air masses, and the character of the landscape changes. Narrow forested valleys give way to broader, drier vales dominated by grasses. Forests are found

Left: Arnica, lupine, false hellebore and red paintbrush wildflowers above Twin Lakes, Crazy Mountains proposed wilderness, Gallatin National Forest

only at the higher elevations of the mountains, which float like islands on a sea of golden grass once grazed by vast herds of bison, elk and bighorn sheep. Today these herds are largely replaced by nonnative cattle and sheep.

Livestock have done more damage to the ecological health of the arid West than any other single human endeavor. The loss of predators, the destruction of watersheds and riparian zones, and the elimination or reduction of competing herbivores, such as bison and elk, are all uncounted costs associated with livestock production. This part of the state has scenic beauty, but because of the demands of the livestock industry, much of the wildness has disappeared along with the wolf, grizzly and bison.

Nevertheless, the land is still grand, and to those who find the northwestern corner's deep woods to be confining, this part of Montana has breadth and width. The eye is set free to gaze upon distant peaks, which frame an even bigger sky. The region's openness is bounded by ranges that give a sense of place, of being rooted by a shoreline of highlands.

It is in these highlands that are found Montana's tallest peaks. The Beartooths, in fact, are one of the most alpine ranges in the lower 48 states, with three-quarters of their land area above treeline. Other lofty highlands include the Madison Range, Gallatin Range, Crazy Mountains, Beaverhead Mountains and Pioneer Mountains, which are the headwaters for such famous trout streams as the Gallatin, Madison, Beaverhead, Big Hole and Yellowstone.

In the center section of the state are isolated uplands — the Little Rockies, Bears Paws, Big Snowies, Little Belts. These surprisingly lush and verdant mountains seem almost adrift on the boundless prairie that characterizes the eastern third of the state.

Then there is the prairie, stretching in rolling bounds all the way east to the Dakotas, interrupted occasionally by abrupt "breaks" along the major rivers, most notably the Missouri and Yellowstone. Many people race across these rolling swells of prairie, seeking to reach the distant shore of mountains to the west or hardwood forests to the east. Yet at one time, this was one of the greatest wildlife pastures on the earth.

In the days of the mountain man, there was no rush to get to the mountains, for the prairie was full of life. Grizzly bear, wolf, bison, elk, bighorn sheep, antelope, prairie dog, goose, prairie chicken and many more species flourished here as nowhere else on the continent. It was a hunter and naturalist's paradise. Then the great herds were killed off and the land was plowed and settled. But the space is still here, and as farming fails in this marginal land of climatic extremes and frequent droughts, people move away, the land slowly heals and some of the wildlife returns.

Perhaps it is because the great herds are gone that some people feel alone here. Perhaps they feel adrift in too much space with no mountains to frame the edge of the universe. For some people, though, this very vastness can have a soothing effect, like that known to sailors on the open sea.

Montanans as a group are not particularly wealthy. We sometimes look with envy at those in other regions who seemingly have everything and are living "the good life." And the way to the good life, we are told, is to mine minerals, cut timber or plow up another quarter section of prairie sod. To my mind, this is a very narrow definition of wealth. For it is not the things that can be possessed or removed that make Montana a wealthy place, but the things that belong to no one, hence everyone. The wildlife legacy enriches everyone in the state, no matter where they live. The uncrowded and still largely uncluttered vistas inspire us, even if we merely sit in our houses and stare out at the snow-covered peaks or rolling prairie.

Montana's dry climate and high elevation impose certain limitations on human endeavors and desires. There are, with few exceptions, better places to grow trees for timber production than in Montana's high, steep mountains. And it's possible to raise more cattle in rainy Georgia than in Montana's arid spaces. We need to ask ourselves the cost in things wild, free and natural of coaxing these commodities from a grudgingly unproductive land. This same land is one of the few places where nature has been so extravagant with scenic splendor and where we can still see the track of a grizzly, hear the autumn bugle of an elk and watch wild trout swim in

Left: Avalanche Creek gorge, Glacier National Park Overleaf: Snow-covered Miller Mountain in the Beartooth Mountains near Cooke City, Gallatin National Forest

water so clear and cold it makes our heads hurt just to look at it. Is this not, in truth, the real wealth of Montana?

To celebrate this elemental quality of wealth, this book is divided into three sections — earth, water and flora. Earth is the foundation upon which all life depends. Water is the substance that binds together all life from tiny amoebae to humankind. And flora is the tapestry of color and form that cloaks the land in a living blanket.

Because I love the Montana landscape, photographing the state is more joy than work. It is a way to capture the symbolic essence of Montana's character and to possess it without depleting it. The images I capture are an attempt to breathe a reality into the dreams that many of us share, providing testimony that beyond the edge of the distant ranges lie more valleys and wild forests, more wild rivers and wildlife. At least for now. But will they last into the next century?

Montana sits at a crossroads. We can either continue to follow the same old tired story of exploitation and waste that has characterized our own history as well as that of so many other places, or we can begin to chart a new path that tries to live with rather than dominate the land.

I am convinced that we need not give up the state's essential character merely to survive. There is room for people as well as for pockets of nature, if we will only learn to coexist. Grizzlies can't live in the heart of our cities, but there is no reason why they can't live in more of our mountains. Bison will never again roam the prairies in uncounted millions, but there is ample room for them to run in herds of countable thousands. There are millions of roadless acres — six million to be exact — that could and should be permanently protected as designated wilderness. Combined with existing designated wilderness, these acres would amount to less than 10 percent of the state. Ninety percent of Montana would continue to be used primarily to serve human development needs. Is 10 percent too much to devote primarily to natural ecological processes and wildlife? I think not.

Preserving the last tattered remnants of what was once a vast Montana landscape is not enough if done in isolation. We also need to restore some battered — but not broken — ecological corridors and pathways. Because many of our roaded lands are lightly developed, there is a chance to reclaim, recover and nurse some of these areas back to ecological health. It will take changes in the way we relate to the land and in what we accept as part of the opportunity we have in living here.

In this state of vast landscapes, it remains to be seen whether we have minds with vast enough imagination to seize the opportunity to become the last best vision of what could be, rather than merely what life has become elsewhere. If we fail — if the last grizzly disappears and the last bison ends up in a zoo and the last wild river is dammed and clear-cuts march up the sides of all of our valleys — an essential element of Montana's character and its people will be destroyed. What we will have gained in material comfort will seem inconsequential compared to what we will have lost.

This book, then, is dedicated to preserving the notion of a wild Montana and the awareness that close proximity to wildlife and wilderness is what makes Montana — and Montanans — different. May it always remain so.

— GEORGE WUERTHNER
Livingston, Montana

Left: Snag on ridge in the Mount Hefty area of the Whitefish Range, North Fork Wildlands proposed wilderness, Flathead National Forest

GEORGE WUERTHNER

MONTANA'S WILDERNESS HISTORY

In some ways, Montana has been at the forefront of the nation's wilderness movement since the first Europeans "discovered" the region we now call the Big Sky Country. "Worthy of our preservation and protection" was artist George Catlin's opinion of the territory's primitive beauty in 1832, after several trips along the Upper Missouri to paint and observe American Indians. Catlin proposed that the government protect such beauty in "a magnificent park, containing man and beast, in all the wildness and freshness of their nature's beauty."

It took a few decades, but Catlin's proposal took form when Yellowstone National Park was created in 1872 to "provide for the preservation . . . of all timber, mineral deposits, natural curiosities, or wonders within said park . . . in their natural conditions."

Shortly before and a couple of decades after the turn of the century, Montana's wildlands lured two other men who would play pivotal roles in the conservation movement. In 1896, Gifford Pinchot, later to become founder and first chief of the U.S. Forest Service, backpacked across what is now Glacier National Park and the Bob Marshall Wilderness and down the Swan Valley. He later celebrated the "beauty and wildness" of the area in his writings.

Pinchot is often unfairly portrayed as having a completely utilitarian approach to forests because he advocated the practice of forestry. But Pinchot recognized that unregulated development threatens wildlands as well as commodity production. He noted, "The West wanted development — wanted it at any cost. What helped development was good, and what hindered it was bad. All other considerations came behind that." Pinchot wanted to temper such reckless pioneer attitudes by employing government management to protect western timberlands. In 1905 he succeeded when the U.S. Forest Service was created.

In 1925 a young Pinchot protégé from the East — Bob Marshall — arrived in Missoula to work for the Forest Service. Young Marshall spent his off-duty hours and vacation time exploring Montana's wildlands, including what would later become the Bob Marshall Wilderness. As a result of these and other early experiences, Marshall went on to become a staunch wilderness advocate.

While working for the Forest Service during the late 1920s and 1930s, Marshall was instrumental in the creation of Forest Service "Primitive Areas," a discretionary designation that recognizes lands with outstanding wildlands characteristics. Many of Montana's finest wildernesses, including the Bob Marshall, Mission Mountains, Cabinet Mountains, Anaconda Pintler, Absaroka-Beartooth and Selway-Bitterroot, were originally set aside as Forest Service Primitive Areas.

While still in his 30s, Marshall founded The Wilderness Society, to act as "an organization of spirited people who will fight for the freedom of the wilderness." Marshall died unexpectedly in 1939, and later the old South Fork Primitive Area was renamed the Bob Marshall Wilderness in honor of his untiring efforts for wilderness preservation.

Forest Service lands remained largely undeveloped until the postwar years of the 1950s, when diminishing timber reserves on private lands brought about an acceleration of timber harvesting on public lands. As more and more once-remote areas were opened up with roads, a group of Montana citizens formed the Montana Wilderness Association (MWA) in 1958 to lobby for protection of federal lands as wilderness.

In its early years, the MWA, along with national organizations such as The Wilderness Society, lobbied for passage of a federal wilderness bill. In 1964 they were successful when the Wilderness Act passed Congress. Instant wilderness status was granted to the Anaconda Pintler, Selway-Bitterroot, Gates of the Mountains, Cabinet Mountains and Bob Marshall wildernesses.

Although the Wilderness Act mandated that all existing primitive areas be studied for potential wilderness designation, there was no specific language about other public lands. The first nonprimitive area in the nation to be designated as wilderness was Montana's Lincoln-Scapegoat Wilderness, setting a precedent as the first citizen-initiated wilderness area.

Preservation efforts for the Scapegoat area had begun in 1962 after citizens learned that the Forest Service was proposing a network of logging roads and clear-cuts in the Lincoln back-country on the southern flank of what would become the Bob Marshall Wilderness in 1964. In 1965 Montana Senators Mike Mansfield and Lee Metcalf introduced legislation to create a 75,000-acre Lincoln-Scapegoat Wilderness.

The Forest Service, though a strong supporter of the wilderness concept in its early days during the 1920s and 1930s, had become increasingly resistant to the wilderness concept by the 1960s. To counter wilderness designation for the Lincoln-Scapegoat area, the agency dropped most of its logging schemes, but proposed building a 75-mile Continental Divide Scenic Highway. To protect the entire back-country area, wilderness advocates enlarged their proposal to 240,000 acres. The proposal was subsequently adopted by Senators Mansfield and Metcalf and submitted to Congress. In 1972 the bill creating the Lincoln-Scapegoat Wilderness passed into law.

With the success of the first citizen-initiated wilderness bill, the MWA began to lobby for other wilderness designations. In 1975 the Mission Mountains, previously a primitive area, were designated as wilderness. In 1976, wilderness designation was enacted for several national wildlife refuge areas, including Red Rock Lakes, UL-Bend and Medicine Lake.

In 1977, acting in response to the inadequacies of a Forest Service roadless area inventory, Senator Metcalf helped pass the Montana Wilderness Study Act. The bill gave protection to nine national forest roadless areas, which the Forest Service had suggested did not possess wilderness qualities. These nine areas included the Taylor-Hilgard portion of what is now the Lee Metcalf Wilderness, plus the Gallatin Range, Blue Joint, West Pioneers, Big Snowy Mountains, Middle Fork Judith, Sapphire Mountains, Mount Henry and Ten Lakes areas. With the exception of Taylor-Hilgard, these other roadless areas still lack any formal wilderness designation at the time of this writing (January 1991).

Montana wilderness supporters had a banner year in 1978. With the support of Senator Metcalf, the Absaroka-Beartooth Wilderness was created when two Forest Service Primitive Areas, the North Absaroka and Beartooth, were joined to make a unified 920,000-acre wilderness, Montana's second largest wilderness after the Bob Marshall.

That same year, citizen efforts to establish the Great Bear Wilderness on the northern end of the Bob Marshall Wilderness were realized when a 286,700-acre wilderness was finalized and enacted into law. The same bill added the Middle Fork of Birch Creek area to the east side of the Bob Marshall, providing the only wilderness protection to the Rocky Mountain Front that exists to date. Another 1978 piece of legislation — the Endangered American Wilderness Bill — also passed Congress, designating 17 new wilderness areas in the West, including the Welcome Creek Wilderness near Missoula.

The year 1980 brought designation of the Rattlesnake Mountains Wilderness, protecting a major roadless area on the doorsteps of Missoula.

In 1983 citizens finally succeeded in getting protection for the Spanish Peaks Primitive Area south of Bozeman. The area had been under proposal for wilderness designation since the formation of the MWA in 1958. Protection came with the passage of the Lee Metcalf Wilderness, named to honor Senator Lee Metcalf, Montana's most ardent congressional wilderness supporter.

Wilderness designation has remained in a quandary since 1983, when the notion of settling the issue of wilderness with a statewide wilderness bill gained political acceptance. In response, the MWA drafted Alternative W, a proposal that identifies most of the major roadless areas in the state for possible wilderness designation. At 2.8 million acres, Alternative W is considered to contain the minimum acreage of the state's remaining 6.5 million roadless acres that could reasonably protect the remainder of Montana's fine wildlands.

Opposition to additional wilderness has been voiced by some Montana citizens and by many extractive industries, including logging, mining and livestock. A number of statewide wilderness bills incorporating portions of Alternative W have been introduced into Congress since 1983, but for one reason or another, all have failed. The latest version was vetoed in late 1988 by then-President Ronald Reagan after it had passed both Houses. As a consequence of the Reagan veto, the future of Montana's wildland heritage remains in limbo. Montana's congressional delegation is likely to continue introducing wilderness legislation, however, resulting in additional wilderness protection for the state.

Over the years many people have contributed to Montana's wilderness preservation efforts, and it is appropriate to recognize at least some of them here: Ken Baldwin, Bob Cooney, John Craighead, Winton Weydemeyer, Grace Miller, George Duvendack, Charles Bradley, John Montagne, Loren Kreck, Les Pengally, Buff Hultman, Ruth Kock, Cecil Garland, Liz Smith, Doris Milner, Joan Montagne, Joe Gaab, Bill Bishop, Beth Miller, Bud Moore, Arnold Bolle, Anne Sutton, Ed Madej, Bill Cunningham, Dale Harris, Rick Gratz, Dale Burk, Cass Chinski, Lou Bruno, Mike Comola, Bob Anderson, Clif Merritt, Olaus Murie, Tom Edwards, Rick Meis, Cary Lund, Mike Bader, Woody Baxter, Howard Kelsey, G.M. Brandborg, Elaine Snyder, Joe Gutkoski, Doug Ferrell, Ed Dobson, Roland Cheek, Keith Shaw, Steward Brandborg, Ken Knudsen, Jim Conner, Cedron Jones, Jim Curtis, Noel Rosetta, Dave Erickson, Smoke Ellis, Bill Leitch, Dick Kuhl, Steve Kelly, Keith Hammer, Lousia Wilcox, Bob Decker, Don Aldrich, John Fredricks, Jim Posewitz, Sandra Cahill, Bob Wagenknecht and John Gatchell. There are undoubtedly other I have missed, but their efforts are not forgotten. Present and future generations owe these citizens a great deal for their tireless efforts to protect Montana's wildland heritage.

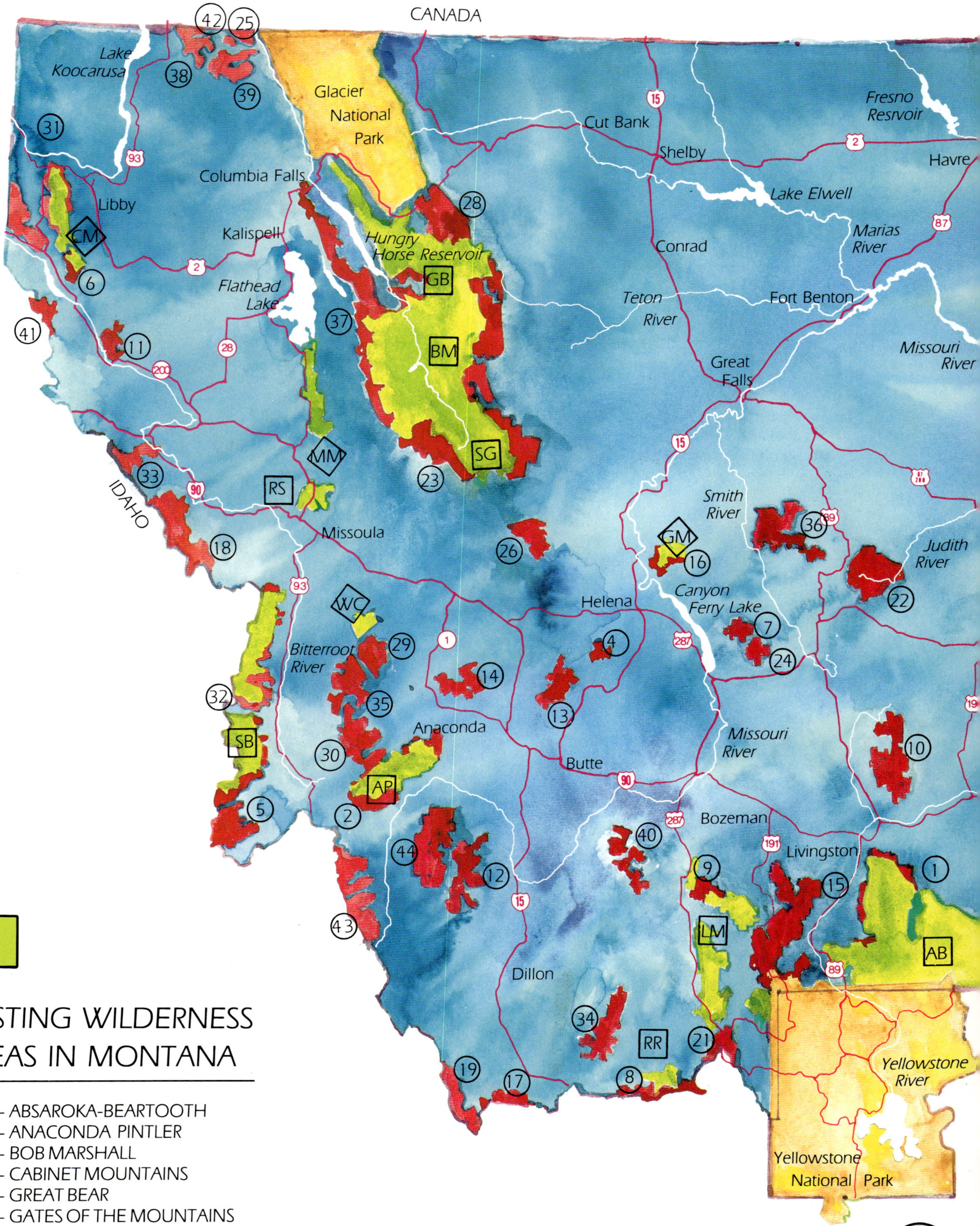

EXISTING WILDERNESS AREAS IN MONTANA

AB — ABSAROKA-BEARTOOTH
AP — ANACONDA PINTLER
BM — BOB MARSHALL
CM — CABINET MOUNTAINS
GB — GREAT BEAR
GM — GATES OF THE MOUNTAINS
LM — LEE METCALF
ML — MEDICINE LAKE
MM— MISSION MOUNTAINS
RR — RED ROCK LAKES
RS — RATTLESNAKE
SB — SELWAY BITTERROOT
SG — SCAPEGOAT
UL — UL BEND
WC — WELCOME CREEK

PROPOSED WILDERNESS AREAS IN MONTANA

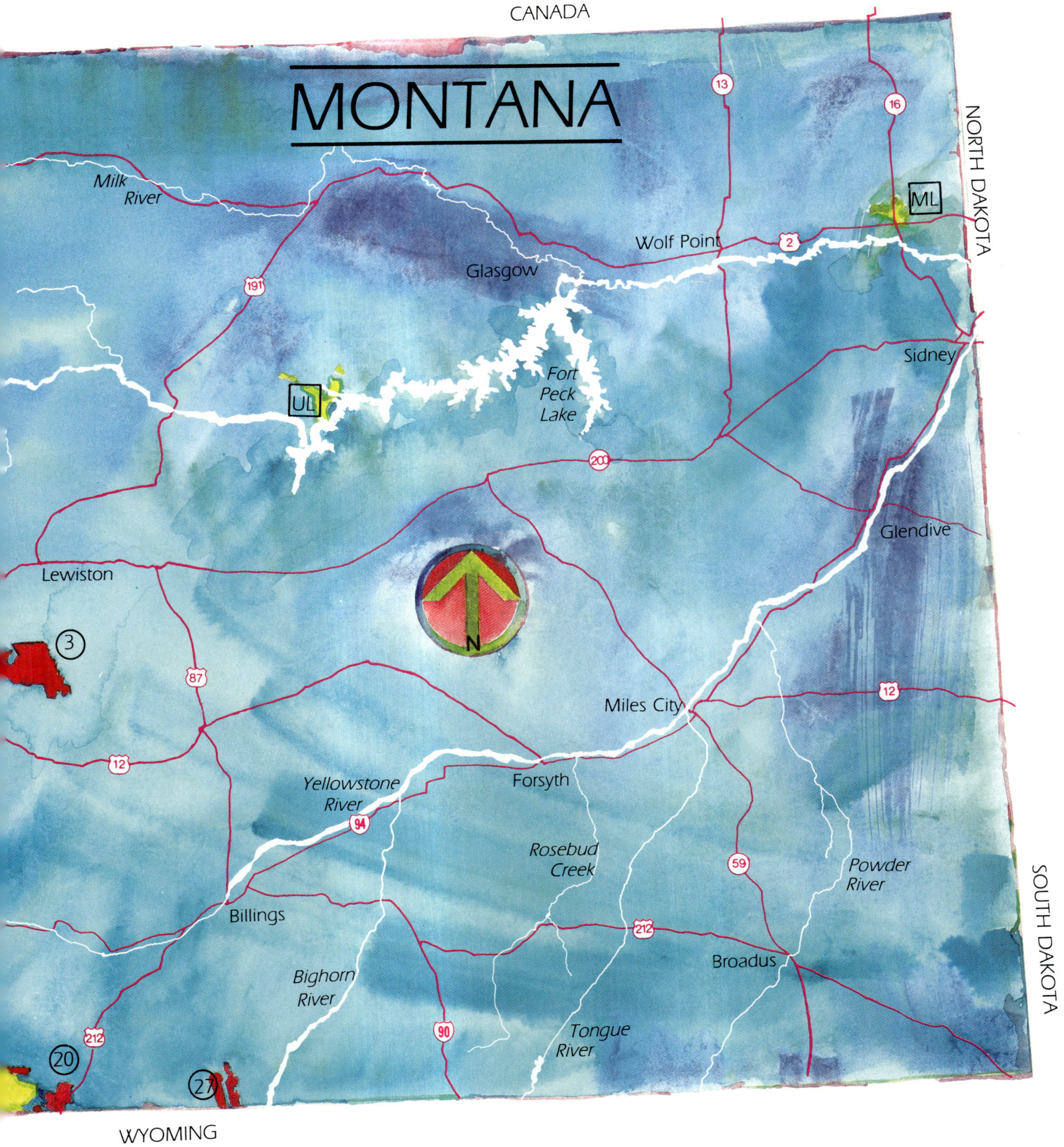

1. ABSAROKA-BEARTOOTH ADDITIONS
2. ANACONDA PINTLER ADDITIONS
3. BIG SNOWY MOUNTAINS
4. BLACK MOUNTAIN
5. BLUE JOINT ADDITION TO THE RIVER OF NO RETURN
6. CABINET MOUNTAIN ADDITIONS
7. CAMAS CREEK
8. CENTENNIAL MOUNTAINS
9. COWBOY HEAVEN ADDITION TO THE LEE METCALF
10. CRAZY MOUNTAINS
11. CUBE IRON–MOUNT SILCOX
12. EAST PIONEERS
13. ELECTRIC PEAK–BLACKFOOT MEADOWS
14. FLINT CREEK RANGE
15. GALLATIN RANGE
16. GATES OF THE MOUNTAIN ADDITION
17. GARFIELD MOUNTAIN
18. GREAT BURN
19. ITALIAN PEAKS
20. LINE CREEK PLATEAU
21. LIONHEAD MOUNTAIN
22. MIDDLE FORK OF THE JUDITH RIVER
23. MONTURE ADDITION TO THE BOB MARSHALL
24. MOUNT BALDY
25. MOUNT HEFTY
26. NEVADA MOUNTAIN
27. PRYOR MOUNTAINS
28. ROCKY MOUNTAIN FRONT ADDITIONS TO THE BOB MARSHALL
29. QUIGG PEAK
30. SAPPHIRE MOUNTAINS
31. SCOTCHMAN PEAKS
32. SELWAY BITTERROOT ADDITIONS
33. SHEEP MOUNTAIN
34. SNOWCREST RANGE
35. STONY MOUNTAIN
36. SMITH RIVER–TENDERFOOT–DEEP CREEK
37. SWAN RANGE ADDITIONS TO THE BOB MARSHALL
38. TEN LAKES
39. THOMPSON SETON
40. TOBACCO ROOT MOUNTAINS
41. TROUT CREEK
42. TUCHUCK
43. WEST BIG HOLE MOUNTAINS
44. WEST PIONEERS

EARTH

Rock seems solid, aloof and eternal. Yet even earth can move, sometimes quite suddenly, as it did in 1959 when the Madison River quake shattered rock along a 10-mile fault and lifted one part of the Madison Range as much as 15 feet higher than the other. In the aftermath of these kinds of chaotic movements, we gain the sublime beauty of crag, peak and summit.

The sense of rigidity we associate with rocks is only illusionary, according to the theory of plate tectonics, for entire continents are moving about as ice floes in a river. This seems appropriate, for there are different levels of perception — we can feel the occasional earthquake, but not the shift of entire continental masses.

Just as plants and animals evolve, there is an evolution of continents, made up of fragments of earlier continents and ocean basins. The Belt Formation, for instance, is formed from sediments laid down as ocean floor more than a billion years ago. Named for the Big Belt Mountains where these rocks were first described, the formation makes up much of northwestern Montana, including the peaks of the Whitefish Range, Swan Range and Glacier National Park.

The granitelike rocks that make up the Beartooth Mountains, Madison Range and other southwestern Montana mountains are more than 3.3 billion years old. The tan limestone cliffs that form prominent "reefs" along the Rocky Mountain Front and elsewhere in the state are all Madison limestone, laid down in ancient, warm seas.

These images of earth are actually sections of geological history. They tell a tale of past wanderings and events that we can still visualize today. In a sense, photography emulates geological formations, for both freeze a particular moment in time, capturing it for others to see. Just as rocks evolve, however, the dyes that make up photographs gradually change over time. Neither art form is permanent, yet each creates the illusion of immutability.

Left: Saint Mary Lake, Glacier National Park Above: Rock mosaic on Monture Creek near Ovando, Monture proposed addition to the Bob Marshall Wilderness, Lolo National Forest

"Everywhere ahead the mountains, the jagged rim where the . . . country joins onto the sky, today were clear and near. A last few desperate patches of snow still showed bright among the topmost clefts of . . . rock, but their destiny was evaporation in another week or so."

— Ivan Doig, *Ride With Me, Mariah Montana*

Glacially formed truncated spurs and horns along Blodgett Creek, Selway-Bitterroot Wilderness proposed additions, Bitterroot National Forest

"The benchlands on either side of the valley road already were beveled pastures of crisp grass; summer in [this] country always takes on a tan by August."

— Ivan Doig, *Ride With Me, Mariah Montana*

Meadows and forest along Nicholia Creek below Italian Peak, Italian Peak proposed wilderness, Beaverhead National Forest

"This was tumbled country. Maybe it took convulsed earth of this kind to produce gold, as had been the case in the Alder Gulch treasure [near] here." — Ivan Doig, *Ride With Me, Mariah Montana*

View north from Sliderock Mountain, Snowcrest Range proposed wilderness, Beaverhead National Forest

Lichen-covered granite boulder along Upper Aero Lake, Absaroka-Beartooth Wilderness, Gallatin National Forest

"Only when our first hour or so of riding carried us above that west edge of the coulee would we see the mountains in total, their broad bases of timber and rockfall gripping into the foothills." — Ivan Doig, *English Creek*

Volcanic rock frames forested slopes of Big Creek, Gallatin Range proposed wilderness, Gallatin National Forest

"I don't know, are mountain reefs general knowledge in the world? I suppose they get their name because they stand as outcroppings do at the edge of an ocean, steady level ridges of stone, as if to give a calm example to the waves beyond them. Except that in this case the blue-gray billow up there is not waves but the Continental Divide against the sky."

— Ivan Doig, *English Creek*

Bird Woman Falls and Mount Oberlin in evening light, Glacier National Park   Overleaf: Clouds and early snow on McPartland Mountain, along McDonald Creek, Glacier National Park

"Accustomed as I was to the . . . concentrated force of the Rocky Mountain Front along a single skyline, here I was surprised by piles of mountain ranges in all directions: the Absarokas to the south, the Castle range to the north, both the Bridger and the Big Belt ranges to the west and northwest, and . . . the high and solitary range called the Crazy Mountains." — Ivan Doig, *Ride With Me, Mariah Montana*

Lenticular clouds over the Crazy Mountains, Crazy Mountains proposed wilderness

"Yet the land still was green where it counted: beside me as I drove, the column of tall old cottonwood trees extending . . . through hay meadow after hay meadow until at last thinning into a pair of willow lines that curved down out of the mountains. . . . " — Ivan Doig, *Ride With Me, Mariah Montana*

Hay meadow below the Centennial Mountains, Centennial Mountains proposed wilderness

"... as we drove along beside [the Bitterroot Valley's] lofty namesake mountains and their attendant canyons, even I could see that here was a piece of country well worth shooting and writing about, fertile valley with ranches and residential areas nervously crowding each other for possession of it. . . . "

— Ivan Doig, *Ride With Me, Mariah Montana*

Along the crest of the Bitterroot Range, from Trapper Peak, Selway-Bitterroot Wilderness, Bitterroot National Forest

Beaverhead Mountains reflect in Harkness Lakes at dawn, Italian Peak proposed wilderness, Beaverhead National Forest

"Wind is the ventriloquism of Montana's seasons. In utter summer it can blow in from the west, the mountains, and convince you November is here. . . .

Snow dusts Sawtooth Ridge in the East Pioneer Mountains, East Pioneers proposed wilderness, Beaverhead National Forest

. . . The other way around, the truly world-changing recital:
the chinook breathing springtime into deadest winter."

— Ivan Doig, *Ride With Me, Mariah Montana*

Spring grasses extend across the Great Plains, near Sand Springs

"Ponderosa (western yellow) pine makes up about one-fifth of Montana's forests. . . . resistant to fire . . . [it] serves a variety of purposes in building houses and ships and in the manufacture of furniture, cars, mine timbers, and railroad ties." — Federal Writers' Project, *Montana*

Ponderosa pine clings to outcrop in the Terry Badlands proposed wilderness, along the Yellowstone River, near Terry

Snow glistens on Republic Mountain in evening light, near Cooke City, Republic Mountain proposed addition to the North Absaroka Wilderness, Gallatin National Forest

"On impulse I drove to the brow of the slope . . . instead of back down to the creek road immediately. As a rancher trying to make a living from this country . . .

East Fork of Little Sheep Creek below Garfield Mountain, Garfield Mountain–Lima Peak proposed wilderness, Beaverhead National Forest

. . . I subscribe to the reminder that view is particularly hard to get a fork into. Yet I somehow didn't want to pass up this divideline chance to sightsee."

— Ivan Doig, *Ride With Me, Mariah Montana*

Unnamed lake below Sheep Mountain, Lionhead proposed wilderness, Gallatin National Forest

Overleaf: Moonrise at sunset over the Continental Divide, Logan Pass area, Glacier National Park

"Behind us the peaks and crags of the Rocky Mountain Front were standing their tallest there at the deepening of evening, while the . . . country around us rested in soft shadows unrolling under that sunset outline of the mountains. This may be my own private theory about such summer evenings but it has always seemed to me that lulls of this sort are how a person heals from the other weather of this land . . .

Looking down the South Fork of the Teton River, Rocky Mountain Front proposed additions to the Bob Marshall Wilderness

. . . for the light calmly going takes with it the grievances that [this] is a country where the wind wears away at you on a daily basis, where drought is never far from happening, where the valley bottoms now in the perfect shirtsleeve climate of summer dusk were thirty-five degrees below zero in the nights of February." — Ivan Doig, *Ride With Me, Mariah Montana*

Granite boulders at Lena Lake, West Big Hole proposed wilderness, Beaverhead National Forest

"The floorlike plain that leads to the foot of the mountains is wet and spongy in some places, in others bone-dry, in still others common prairie. . . . kindred promontories make a line of landmarks between the mountains and the eastward horizon of plains. . . . they remind me of lighthouses, spaced as they are along the edge of that tumult of rock that builds into the Continental Divide. Lone sentinel forms the eye seeks." — Ivan Doig, *Ride With Me, Mariah Montana*

Sunset over the Missouri River, Charles M. Russell National Wildlife Refuge

Eroded sandstone near Nelson Creek, Charles M. Russell National Wildlife Refuge

"If a person can take time to reflect on such a reach of land other matters will dim out. . . . A hawk went by below us, sailing on an air current. A mark of progress into the mountains I always watched for, hawks and even eagles now on routes lower than our own." — Ivan Doig, *English Creek*

Rainbow Lake and West Goat Peak, Anaconda Pintler Wilderness

"What a daystarting view it must be from [the firetower], out over the spread city and this broad shallow bowl of cultivated valley and the clasping ring of mountains all around." — Ivan Doig, *Ride With Me, Mariah Montana*

Alpine wildflowers and boulders on Mount Edith in the Big Belt Mountains, Mount Baldy proposed wilderness, Helena National Forest

WATER

Montana is a dry place. It's not quite a desert in the traditional sense, with cactus and Gila monsters, but like most of the West it just barely avoids the desert classification. It is only because of the mountains — those snow-trapping heights that provide a year-round flow to the lowlands — that any of the state is inhabitable at all.

In the highest and wettest areas, such as Logan Pass in Glacier National Park, there can be as much as 120 inches of annual precipitation. To give some notion of what this means, consider that rainy Seattle gets about 38 inches annually. Most Montana communities, located as they are in the valleys, are lucky if they get more than 12 to 14 inches a year. Some parts get less. Dillon, surrounded by high mountain ranges, has the distinction as the driest place in Montana, with a scant 9.5 inches recorded in the average year. This qualifies as genuine desert.

It is not surprising, then, that water is so attractive to those of us who live in Montana. We love our rivers, our waterfalls, our lakes. Water, with its magical qualities, is the focus of all life here.

If earth seems immovable and stoic, water is the language of earth. Splashing down rock ledges, cascading through gorges, dripping from needles, falling into the winter hush as snow, water talks to us in its many forms and manifestations.

For a photographer, water is always a welcome subject. It can be captured as silver as it threads down a waterfall, or gold or red as it traps the reflection of evening sky or sun-colored rock. Water can be shaped by the earth as it gushes through a rocky gorge or freezes into an icy sculpture. Water can also shape the earth: water-rounded boulders line our streams; soft clays erode to create exotic badlands; and glacial ice scours, plucks and smooths mountains.

Water is one of nature's most mutable — and most beautiful — expressions.

Left: Pine Creek Lake outlet below Mount Black, Absaroka-Beartooth Wilderness, Gallatin National Forest Above: Autumn colors along the shore of Echo Lake in the Swan Range, Swan proposed additions to the Bob Marshall Wilderness

"Forests, by increasing the absorptive power of the soil, retard the runoff of moisture when snow is melting in the spring, prevent erosion, and decrease the amount of silt carried into streams and reservoirs. The shade prevents rapid evaporation in summer, allowing rain to soak into the ground and augment the supply of ground water, a very real factor in maintaining the flow of streams and springs."

— Federal Writers' Project, *Montana*

Reflections at Sylvan Lake, Kootenai National Forest

Winter sunset on the Wild and Scenic section of the Missouri River, Charles M. Russell National Wildlife Refuge

Shoreline of Horseshoe Lake, Absaroka-Beartooth Wilderness, Gallatin National Forest

Mill Falls on the South Fork of the Teton River, Rocky Mountain Front proposed additions to the Bob Marshall Wilderness, Lewis and Clark National Forest

"The annual flow of Montana's rivers, with their sources in the great national forests, is sufficient to cover the whole State with six inches of water — more than enough to irrigate ten million acres. It does not drain off in great floods — for snow at the higher altitudes melts slowly — but assures a flow throughout the summer." — Federal Writers' Project, *Montana*

Rushing waters of Rattlesnake Creek, Rattlesnake National Recreation Area

Silver Staircase framed by spring foliage along Highway 2, Flathead National Forest
Overleaf: Sunrise on Lower Aero Lake in the Beartooth Mountains, Absaroka-Beartooth Wilderness, Gallatin National Forest

"It still floors me, how the mountains are not the same any two days in a row. As if hundreds of copies of those mountains exist and each dawn brings in a fresh one, of new color, new prominence of some feature over the others, a different wrapping of cloud or rinse of sun for this day's version." — Ivan Doig, *English Creek*

McDonald Peak in the Mission Mountains Tribal Wilderness, Flathead Indian Reservation, from Ninepipe National Wildlife Refuge

Gorge along the Dearborn River, Rocky Mountain Front proposed additions to the Bob Marshall Wilderness, Lewis and Clark National Forest

"It starts, early in the mountain summer, far back among the high spilling slopes. . . . The single sound is hidden water . . . diving down its willow-masked gulch. The stream flees north through this secret and peopleless land until . . . a bow of meadow makes the riffled water curl wide to the west. At this interruption, a low rumple of the mountain knolls itself up watchfully. . . . " — Ivan Doig, *This House of Sky*

Family Peak and the North Fork of Birch Creek, Badger–Two Medicine area, Rocky Mountain Front proposed additions to the Bob Marshall Wilderness, Lewis and Clark National Forest

Waterfall along the East Fork of Rock Creek, Big Snowy Mountains proposed wilderness, Lewis and Clark National Forest

"Montana's streams and rivers make sense of her geography, give relief to her topography, and define her settlements. People do not inhabit Montana as such; they inhabit the Madison Valley, the Bitterroot Valley, and the Gallatin Valley." — Jan Konigsberg, *Montana Spaces*

Boulders punctuate the waters of the Blackfoot River, near Greenough

Falls above Hidden Lake, Glacier National Park

"This far up the [creek] didn't amount to much. Most places you could cross it in a running jump. But the stream was headed down out of the mountains in a hurry and so had some pretty riffles and every now and again a pool like a big wide stairstep of glass. If fish weren't in one of those waters, they were in the other." — Ivan Doig, *English Creek*

Grasses along Rock Creek, a Blue Ribbon trout stream in Lolo National Forest, eastern border of the Welcome Creek Wilderness

Forest and fallen trees along the West Fork of Rock Creek, Sapphire Mountains proposed wilderness, Deerlodge National Forest

"Up and up I and my horses and my dreams went, toward the angle of slope. . . . Eventually a considerable sidehill of timber took the trail from sight, and before Pony and Bubbles and I entered the stand of trees, I whoaed us for a last gaze along all the mountains above and around. They were the sort of thing you would have if every cathedral in the world were lined up along the horizon." — Ivan Doig, *English Creek*

Misty morning along McDonald Creek below the Garden Wall, Glacier National Park

Kootenai Falls on the Kootenai River west of Libby, Kootenai National Forest   Overleaf: Wild roses in bloom along the banks of the Missouri River, Charles M. Russell National Wildlife Refuge

"That is the pattern the seasons make in this part of the [country], a north-facing slope bursting with trees and brush because snow stays longest there and provides moisture, while a south-facing slope is timberless but grassy because of all the sun it gets." — Ivan Doig, *English Creek*

Pond in the Flathead Valley, near Creston

Mosses along Big Spring Creek, Snowcrest Range proposed wilderness, Beaverhead National Forest

"There's enough space in the state, and few enough people; everyone might well have a favorite view all to themselves and never have to share it with another. The urgency of space is something that is shared, yet remains intensely personal. It's an intimate link with the landscape you carry with you when you live in Montana, or live away from it. — Glenn Law, *Montana Spaces*

Skalkaho Falls in the Sapphire Mountains, Stoney Mountain proposed wilderness, Bitterroot National Forest

Reeds along the Little Bighorn River, near Crow Agency

"Winter, long white winter. Then a pale quick sprig of spring. Then unsteady too-hot-too-damp-too-dry summer. Next an overnight autumn, and suddenly the breadth of winter once more." — Ivan Doig, *This House of Sky*

Gardiner River in winter sunshine, Yellowstone National Park, Montana-Wyoming border

Reeds along the Yellowstone River at Coulson Park, Billings

FLORA

Cloaking the land and giving it texture, color and smell is the floral component. Montana is rich in floral variety, from the cactus and yucca of the honey-colored plains to the resonant greens of the hemlock, devil's club and ferns of the northwestern forests.

Flora provides a palette of colors throughout the year. Spring brings the lush greens of cottonwood bottoms. In summer there are the vibrant turquoise of alpine forget-me-nots and the rosy hues of purple mountain saxifrage, as these tiny alpine wildflowers lodge between boulders and rocks on the highest peaks. Each fall entire hillsides of aspen and larch blaze with the boldness of gold. In winter there is the rich, seasoned rufous glow of weathered treeline snags against snow.

The variety of plant communities found in Montana is the result of many elements — weather, rock and ecological processes such as fire. Each influences what will grow where. In a way, flora tells a story much as earth, but it is a more immediate tale that reflects conditions of the present and the recent past.

Each type of flora is a page in the naturalist's notebook. Doghair stands of lodgepole pine tell of a forest fire decades ago. Prickly pear cactus suggests thin and rocky soils. Limber pine is almost always evidence of soils with a high calcium content, such as those found on Madison limestone formations.

The land's vegetation enlivens more senses than sight and intellectual curiosity. The scent of fresh cottonwood leaves signals the return of spring. The sting of nettles against bare legs speaks of hot summer days. Aspen leaves rustling in the breeze are a hint of fall. And the wind sweeping through winter-bare branches of alpine larch whistles a lonesome chorus to the highest peaks.

Left: Leafy spurge in Smith River Canyon near Tenderfoot Creek, Smith River–Tenderfoot proposed wilderness   Above: Crown Butte, Daisy Pass and whitebark pines, Gallatin National Forest

"And of course one of the things a person always does a lot of in Montana is watching other people's weather. All that sky and horizon around you, there almost always is some atmospheric event to keep track of." — Ivan Doig, *English Creek*

Aspen near Black Butte, Gravelly Range proposed wilderness, Beaverhead National Forest

Balsamroot and the Absaroka Mountains near Livingston, Tie Creek proposed addition to the Absaroka-Beartooth Wilderness, Gallatin National Forest   Overleaf: Yellowstone River, near Columbus

"

. . . beauty makes the eyes greedy. For even after all this, mountains and moon and earth edges and the coming of the sun, I considered that what was most worth watching for was the first shadow of the day. When the sun worked its way about half above the horizon, that shadow emerged to stretch itself . . . into an apparition of leftover dark a couple of hundred feet in length." — Ivan Doig, *English Creek*

Fresh snow along Trout Creek near Superior, Great Burn proposed wilderness

Western red cedar and serviceberry, Cabinet Mountains Wilderness, Kootenai National Forest

"The montane group includes most of the coniferous forests, and ranges from the lower border of the subalpine to the valley grasslands. . . . In the moister parts of the lower montane forest are Moneses and prince's pine, lowland and Douglas fir, and western larch. . . ." —Federal Writers' Project, *Montana*

Western larch blaze on a hillside near Trail Creek, Whitefish Range, Flathead National Forest

Devil's club at Ross Creek Cedars Scenic Area, Scotchman Peak proposed wilderness, Kootenai National Forest

"The subalpine group, characterized by plants that appeared after the recession of the glaciers . . . has made the higher altitudes in the northern Rockies famous for their profusion of color in the short midsummer season. When the snowbanks melt and all the flowers bloom at once, the earth is brilliant. . . ." — Federal Writers' Project, *Montana*

Lupine below Eighteen Mile Peak, Beaverhead Mountains, Italian Peak proposed wilderness

Alpine sunflowers on South Baldy Mountain, Tobacco Root Mountains proposed wilderness, Beaverhead National Forest Overleaf: Western larch frames the Middle Fork of the Flathead River, looking toward Glacier National Park

"Subsurface moisture encourages stream bank forests composed largely of cottonwood and aspen, but often containing alders, river birches, willow, and the like."

— Federal Writers' Project, *Montana*

Cottonwoods along Six Mile Creek below Emigrant Peak, Emigrant Peak proposed addition to the Absaroka-Beartooth Wilderness

Whitebark pine frames Twin Lakes below Stuart Peak, Rattlesnake Mountains Wilderness, Lolo National Forest

"

. . . [we] passed by a parcel of the Custer National Forest
that consisted of chalk buttes and some scattered ponderosa
pine. . . . those of us [rangers] stationed out here used to joke
that maybe the Custer wasn't the biggest national forest . . .
but it . . . was the longest. Across about seven hundred miles
. . . the Custer was a scatter of administrative islands
of dry stands of forest or grasslands."

— Ivan Doig, *Ride With Me, Mariah Montana*

Ponderosa pine near Whitetail Cabin, Ashland Ranger District, Custer National Forest

Cottonwood along the Yellowstone River, Paradise Valley

"... the Flathead Valley stretched like a green tile floor, farms and ranches out across the level earth in highly orderly fashion ... and to the east the Mission Mountains tepeed up prettily in single long slants of slope from the valley floor to peaks a mile and a half high." — Ivan Doig, *Ride With Me, Mariah Montana*

Meadow near the Middle Fork of the Flathead River Valley, with Great Northern Peak in the distance, Great Bear Wilderness

Cottonwood leaves among pine needles on Ranch Creek, Quigg Peak proposed wilderness, Lolo National Forest

Beargrass frames Bluebird Lake in the Ten Lakes Scenic Area, Ten Lakes proposed wilderness, Kootenai National Forest

Indian paintbrush blooms in the Mount Edith area of the Big Belt Mountains, Mount Baldy proposed wilderness, Helena National Forest

"Montana has a tattered side. You look at the blowing away prairies that never should have been cut by a plow and the little towns they are taking with them, you look at the dump heaps and earth poisons left by mining, you look at so many defeated lives on the Indian reservations . . . you look at these warps in Montana and they add up in a hurry to a hundred years of pretty sad behavior."

— Ivan Doig, *Ride With Me, Mariah Montana*

Alpine larch on Carlton Ridge, Selway-Bitterroot Wilderness

Ponderosa pine in the Gates of the Mountains Wilderness, Helena National Forest
Overleaf: Cottonwood along the Tongue River, near Miles City

Yellow columbine along Beaver Creek, Lee Metcalf Wilderness

Prickly pear cactus in bloom at the Missouri Breaks, Charles M. Russell National Wildlife Refuge

"Then you draw a deep breath, get a little of this endemic fresh air sweeping through your brain . . . and you look at the valleys that are the green muscles on the rock bones of this state, you look at the last great freeflowing river in the continental U.S., the Yellowstone. . . . "

— Ivan Doig, *Ride With Me, Mariah Montana*

Quaking aspen in the Spanish Peaks area of Gallatin National Forest, Lee Metcalf Wilderness

Old snag above a cirque lake in the West Fork of Fish Creek drainage, Great Burn proposed wilderness, Lolo National Forest

"

. . . you look at people who've been perpetually game to outwork the levels of pay here because they can love a mountain with their eyes while doing it, you look at the unbeatable way the land latches into the sky here atop the Rocky Mountain Front or on the curve of the planet across the eastern plains — and you end up calculating that our first hundred years [of statehood] could have been spent worse."

— Ivan Doig, *Ride With Me, Mariah Montana*

Penstemon near Bluebird Lake, Ten Lakes proposed wilderness, Kootenai National Forest

Fire-killed snags above the Middle Fork of Birch Creek, Rocky Mountain Front, Bob Marshall Wilderness

Birch leaves and larch needles cover rotting log, Great Bear Wilderness

Whitebark pine on Bobcat Mountain, West Pioneers proposed wilderness, Beaverhead National Forest

Technical Information

The photographic images for this book were made with a Calumet 4x5 view camera and lenses varying from 75mm to 300mm. Some closeup work was done with 35mm Nikon cameras and lenses.

Exposures were calculated with a Sekonic incident light meter. Lens apertures ranged from f/16 to f/64 with shutter speeds between 1/15 of a second to as long as 10 seconds.

Ektachrome and Fujichrome professional daylight transparency films were used for all the 4x5 work. Kodachrome 25 and 64 daylight films were used for the 35mm work.

Acknowledgements

I'd like to thank the many men and women who have tirelessly and unselfishly given of their time, money and hearts to protect and preserve Montana's wilderness heritage, not only so I can photograph these special places, but so that generations yet unborn may also know what I have been so privileged to experience. To each and every one I owe a debt of gratitude.

— G.W.

Beargrass blooms in the Swan Range, Jewel Basin proposed addition to the Bob Marshall Wilderness, Flathead National Forest